SILLY SEALS

Karen Morgan

Down East Books
Camden, Maine
Guilford, Connecticut

Down East Books

An imprint of Globe Pequot

Distributed by NATIONAL BOOK NETWORK

Photos by On the Mark Wildlife Photography on pp. 6, 10, 14, 18, 24, 31, 34, 36, 40, 48, 52, 54, 58, 60, 66, 76, 84, 88, 110, and 122
Photos by Steve De Neef Photography on pp. 8, 12, 16, 20, 27, 28, 32, 38, 44, 46, 50, 56, 62, 64, 70, 72, 74, 78, 80, 86, 90, 96, 100, 104, 108, 114, 116, and 124

British Library Cataloguing in Publication Information available

Library of Congress Cataloging-in-Publication Data available

ISBN 978-1-60893-976-3 (hardcover)
ISBN 978-1-60893-977-0 (e-book)

♾™ The paper used in this publication meets the minimum requirements of American National Standard for Information Sciences—Permanence of Paper for Printed Library Materials, ANSI/NISO Z39.48-1992.

Printed in China

This book is dedicated to my dad, who made us laugh in church and got us all in trouble.

Oh, hi there.

I'm just getting a little snack.

It's totally on my diet.

George, I told you all the
good seats would be taken
if we didn't hurry. But no,
you had to stop for squid.

Ever so gracefully, Jessica balanced on the tip of her flipper. Her underwater ballet classes had finally paid off.

Honey, wake up. What have I told you about having too much mackerel in the afternoon?

I think Freddy needs new glasses. He's been talking to that seaweed for an hour.

Yes, Junior, I see the nude beach. No, those people don't have any clothes on. Yes, I'm sure they are cold. Especially that man on the left.

I know I dropped my
car keys here somewhere.

My mom said I had to eat all my vegetables before I can have dessert. I think we're gonna be here a while.

I'm so glad we were able
to get tickets to
Cirque du Seal-eil!

Oh, hey, Mom.
Remember when you told
me not to climb down here
or I would get stuck?

Calgon seaweed,
take me away.

Do you think this is the right shade
to make my eyes pop?

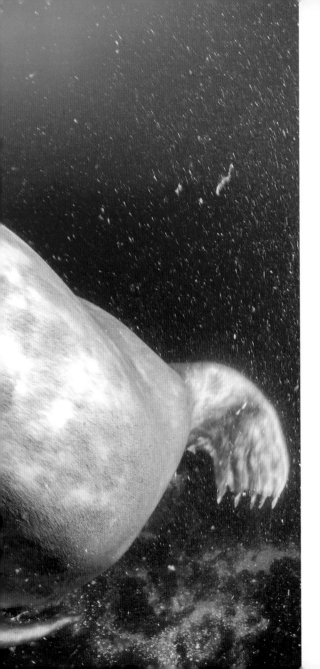

Why do they call us sea dogs when we have these beautiful kitty whiskers?

You didn't hear this from me,
but Linda said Jackie told her that Monica was
having some work done on her whiskers.

Herman was just a
little bit off-kilter.

SEAL Team Six minus Five sneaks up on the unsuspecting floating seaweed.

Today was little
Johnny's birthday party.
We all had way too much cake.

If you hold your breath
and count to twenty,
it feels like you are
floating in the ocean.

Seal staring contest! Go!
One, two, three, four, five
. . . one thousand. I win!

Seriously, Donald.
What did you eat for lunch?

That awkward moment when you wave to someone you thought was waving to you—but wasn't.

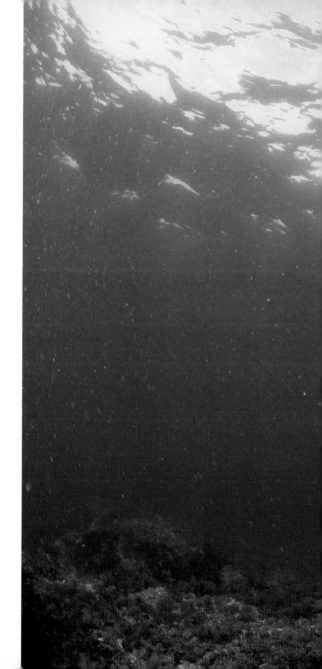

Advanced Yoga Pose #13:

"Upside-Down Underwater

Downward-Facing Sea Dog"

The girls at Seaweed Pilates grew tired of Samantha's showing off.

Excuse me, but I seem to be lost. I'm trying to find the Cute Sea Creature Convention.

I'm not saying you're dumb, Freddy. But if I stare really hard, I can see through your head all the way to Nova Scotia.

I'm following.

I'm being followed.

I'm following.

I'm being followed.

Mabel tried waxing, plucking, even electrolysis. But she couldn't get rid of those stubborn whiskers.

Ugh! I forgot you're supposed to bring in the class snack tomorrow. How many pups are in your pod? I hope no one is allergic to shellfish.

Marjorie and the girls began
to have second thoughts about
the all-you-can-eat buffet.

After a very long Maine winter,
Larry was looking forward
to working on his tan.

Ooh! I think something
just touched my tail!

Sandy was a cute seal, but she laughed like a walrus and rarely had a second date.

I just bought these luxurious 800-count seaweed sheets. They are simply mahvelous!

"Nnneeaoowww!
I'm an airplane!"

You can't even tell that
I've been eating garlic
on my mackerel.

Hey, Mom, wake up!
There's a guy here who says
he's looking for french fries.

And the Great White Seal
said unto them, "Be not afraid.
For behold, I bring you tidings
of great joy and mackerel."

My wife decided we would
go vegan. So now I only
eat plants like these.
Do you have any fish?
We don't need to tell her.

Are you a fruit?
Because Honeydew you know
how fine you look right now?

As Neville climbed up on the seaweed, he realized the seal party was in fact just a bunch of rocks.

Maybe she's born with it.
Maybe it's mackerel.

Bwahahaha!
Joke's on you, Seagull.
Those weren't really
french fries.

Then we stretch our right
flipper to the sky,
slowly moving into a half-
moon pose while we breathe
and say, "Namaste."

I say, old chap,
is this the way to the
English Channel?

It's called a side plank.
It's great for your core
and makes you want to
go drink margaritas.

If you yell "Geronimo!"
when you jump,
the belly flop doesn't
hurt as much.

Whatever floats your boat!

Seal selfies are the best!
If you tilt your head to
the right, your whiskers
look much prettier.

Daily Seal Affirmation #4:
I am happy and confident,
and my flippers are strong.

Mrs. Johnson bobbed innocently in her inflatable swim ring, unaware that her life was about to change forever.

Out of my way, girls.
I am the new Esther Williams!

As Valerie swam past,
we could tell she was still
angry about the mackerel
casserole incident.

The other seals tried to tell
Henrietta about deodorant,
but she refused to listen.

Benjamin "forgot his wallet" again,
so he asked the guys to spot him a few clams.

I know I came into
this room for a reason.
Maybe if I swim away and
come back in again,
I'll remember why.

Pee-eww!
I think it's time to buy
a new pair of flippers.

Hey, Mike, heads up.
Cute cows at four o'clock.
Come on, man, suck it in.

Robert went for the high five. Got left hanging.

Don't turn around now, Marjorie, but Reginald is checking out your hind flippers.

Now I lay me down to sleep;
I pray for mackerel to eat.

How many times have I told him—
those swim trunks don't fit him anymore.